Stephen Bayley

Design Classics

The Lucky Strike Packet
by Raymond Loewy

Verlag form

Raymond Loewy's career was a gloriously bright comet of novelty whose tail comprised items of flashy coruscating kitsch mixed indiscriminately with genuine solid achievement. It is no surprise that Loewy's career almost exactly parallels the growth of the advertising and public relations businesses in New York. His star was fast rising on a curve of professionalism (whose radius bore his own unmistakable signature).

Hitherto there were 'commercial artists'. Indeed, Loewy's own career began as a humble window dresser in Fifth Avenue stores. Then Loewy invented himself as one of the first professional design consultants: the semantics are significant. The passage from artisan to professional reflects both the rising status of industrial design and the growth of consumerism. The distinctive contribution of Raymond Loewy did much to develop each.

Significantly, Loewy used the first professional publicists with appropriate commitment. The motto of the publicists was Benjamin Sonnenberg's "always live better than your clients". Loewy made his clients look better than their competitors (and, incidentally, always looked better than his clients himself). His mother had told him "better be envied than pitied" and Loewy never neglected an opportunity to impress his clients or his public. His image is indistinguishable from his achievements. He often sounded better than his PR and sold himself better than his advertising agency. His best bit of design was, of course, himself. Every designer working today owes his status to the professional adventure Loewy began when he opened his first office in New York in 1927.

It's almost impossible to disentangle substance from symbol in assessing Raymond Loewy and in its paradoxical way that is evidence of his extraordinary contribution to twentieth century material culture. In a century when image has assumed quantifiable material value (and trivialised the economic significance of actual manufacturing), Loewy was one of a handful of individuals (which includes W.D. Teague, Brooks Stevens, Harley Earl and Virgil Exner) whose taste defined and directed mid-century America, providing the world's richest citizens with products, services and symbols which met all their needs. In the hands of Raymond Loewy design became not a

matter of morals (as it was, say, for the Arts and Crafts Movement), but a question of cultural modelling and social competition and, of course, the stimulation of consumption.

It has often been said that circa 1950 the average American could have spent his entire day in contact with consumer goods and services of Loewy's devising. A *Schick* razor and *Pepsodent* toothpaste in the morning. A ride to work in the family *Studebaker*, or a trip on a *Greyhound* bus. An ice cold beverage from a *Coke* dispenser for lunch. A *Carling* beer in the cinq-à-sept. And of course, a cigarette. Perhaps the most complete symbol of achievement in a career of winning symbolism was the *Lucky Strike* packet. In all its brightness, triviality, insubstantiality, vigour and enduring success it's a perfect microcosm of American design in its heroic years. It's also the perfect Loewy signature. In *Lucky Strike* you find the winning combination of a confident eye in the service of very big business. Is it a masterpiece of graphic design? No. Is it typical of Loewy's achievement as a professional designer? Certainly. Does it show how design helped create brands and, thus, the heraldry of the century? Absolutely!

There are many things which distinguish American from European culture, especially the character of feeling. English speakers know from schooldays Thomas Gray's sublimely melancholic *Elegy in a Country Churchyard*. The American is more likely to know Christopher Morley's (1890-1957) parody of it, *Elegy Written in a Country Coal Bin*:

Streamline, steam and speed: Loewy with the 6000 PS locomotive S 1, which he designed in 1938 for the Pennsylvania Railroad Company.

Full many a can of purest kerosene
The dark unfathomed tanks of Standard Oil
Shall furnish me, and with their aid I mean
To bring my morning coffee to a boil.

In four spare lines you have a nice summary of a culture. Note the introduction of a brand name (Standard Oil), the bathetic reference to industrial fuels (kerosene) and the tone of good-natured mockery.

Comparisons of transatlantic achievement in design are equally telling. The austere Hannes Meyer, interim director of the *Bauhaus*, believed that all life could be explained in terms of hydrocarbons and right angles. It is not recorded that Hannes Meyer had a sense of frivolity or was much animated by the pleasures of luxury. To Loewy the most beautiful thing in the world was that upwardly rising sales curve. The European designer of the twenties wanted nothing more than to develop the perfect cantilevered tubular steel chair which would stand as an exemplar for all time: an algorithm of technology and taste. The contemporary American designer wanted nothing more than to make a few thousand dollars in the period that Scott Fitzgerald called the greatest, gaudiest spree in history.

It was Americans who developed the concept of planned obsolescence (although at the time they called it 'the dynamic economy'). Nothing can be more contrary to the European vision, which goes back to Plato, that design is about the pursuit of perfect and unchanging standards. Of course, in the twentieth century each culture respected mass-production. Le Corbusier believed

Rounded forms and yet sharp: the *Studebaker Commander* convertible, designed in 1950 by Loewy.

that mass-production required standards and that these standards led to perfection. The American designer saw mass-production as an economic tool, a sort of creative supercharger, a commission multiplier.

Look at a photograph of Raymond Loewy and you can see the white suit, the extravagant foulard and you can almost smell the eau-de-cologne, the pomade and sense the suntan. His studio was not the frozen atelier of a tortured and consumptive artist, but a warm country club lounge. This is not Dessau or Weissenhof, it's Park Avenue or Palm Springs.

"It's toasted" – the self-understood as something special (1926).

Virginia Gold

In the history of US consumerism, *Lucky Strike* is almost as significant as *Coca-Cola*. The comparisons are revealing: a product intended to achieve a stable monopoly in a turbulent market, driven and developed by a client with a messianic commitment to the product who exploited the available skills of 'marketing services' (which is to say, design, PR and advertising) to the utmost.

Like "paydirt" and "cheapskate", the expression "lucky strike" comes from the Californian Gold Rush of 1849. Pure Americana. When gold was found on Swiss emigré Joseph Sutter's Nueva Helvetia land grant territory in what we now call the Sacramento Valley, California was – literally – put on the map. Hitherto neglected and deserted, a very native form of opportunistic avarice – a hostile critic would call it money-grubbing – created the Sunshine State. We can name the very day: it was 28th February 1849 when the steamboat *California* deposited the first 49ers in La Villa Real de Santa Fe de San Francisco de Asis. [1] They were in search of lucky strikes.

The context of the *Lucky Strike* brand was the creation of the US cigarette industry with all its associations of monopoly, imaginative promotions and global spread. In 1911 the giant old American Tobacco Company (ATC), established by James Buchanan Duke 21 years before, was broken-up by anti-trust legislation into three new companies: new ATC, Liggett & Myers and P. Lorillard. Their prominent consumer products were Turkish style cigarettes, under the respective ethnic brands *Omar*, *Fatima* and *Zebelda*. At this time, only R. J. Reynolds was energetically committed to a Virginia tobacco cigarette, its unsuccessful *Reyno*.

The first modern cigarette was *Camels*, launched in Cleveland, 1913, by the R. J. Reynolds Company. Innovation was not just nationwide marketing and distribution and thereby the establishment of what later became known as a 'Standard Brand', but the more sinister gustatory achievement of blending burley and Turkish tobaccos in a manner that allowed smokers to inhale without coughing, something which the older blends and brands could not guarantee. In this way the Supreme Court later said that *Camels* "revolutionised the tobacco industry" [2]. Hitherto a cigarette was an exotic product made of Turkish tobacco. It was favoured by artists and eccentrics: Oscar Wilde says in *Dorian Gray* (1890): "A cigarette is the perfect type of perfect pleasure. It is exquisite, and it leaves one unsatisfied. What more can one want?"

Santa Claus serving the tobacco industry. Advertising poster for the green pack at the end of the thirties.

"Luckies are easy on my throat"

From Laughs to Tears in 30 Seconds

CLAUDETTE COLBERT tells how the throat-strain of emotional acting led her to Luckies...

"Emoting to order" is certainly a real strain on the throat. That's why an actress thinks twice before choosing a cigarette. Miss Colbert says: "After experimenting, I'm convinced that my throat is safest with Luckies."

Ask a tobacco expert why Luckies are so easy on the throat. He'll undoubtedly explain that the choice tobacco Lucky Strike buys, makes for a light smoke. And he may add that the exclusive "Toasting" process takes out certain irritants found in *all* tobacco.

Here's the experts' actual verdict...Sworn records show that, among independent tobacco experts not connected with *any* cigarette manufacturer, Luckies have twice as many exclusive smokers as all other brands combined.

Sworn Records Show That... **WITH MEN WHO KNOW TOBACCO BEST – IT'S LUCKIES 2 TO 1**

Copyright 1938, The American Tobacco Company

But Camels was a modern blend, packaged and promoted accordingly. In its first year there was an advertising budget of 1,5 million US dollars. R. J. Reynolds assiduously used promotions to increase its marketshare. You did not simply buy a packet of cigarettes, you might also be given a Yale pennant, a miniature oriental rug, a map of Portugal or a portrait of Lillian Russell. *Camels* soon became a sales phenomenon and market leader.

George Washington Hill, pugnacious scion of the American Tobacco Company dynasty whose career had begun in the leaf markets of Wilson, NC, at first thought *Camels* "a joke", but he soon came to realise that *Camels'* success meant the end of the old-fashioned Turkish style cigarettes and signified that the market of the future was for Virginia blends. He started searching for a brand whose resonance would rival the straightforward clarity of *Camels* and found that ATC's Dr R.A. Patterson of Richmond, VA, had as long ago as 1871 already put *Lucky Strike* into the company's portfolio of registered brands... as a name for pipe-smoking plug tobacco.

Lucky Strike cigarettes were test-marketed in 1916 in Buffalo, in upper New York State, and went nationwide in 1917. The advertising emphasised the flavoursome tobacco blends with the strapline "It's Toasted" (although it's worth pointing out that all cigarette tobacco is toasted). In the days when advertising agencies could get away with literal illustrations, the first ads actually showed a piece of toast pierced by a fork. By the end of the first year of sales, *Luckies* had 11% share. This modest expressive effort was the beginning of what, at the time,

Claudette Colbert: convinced of the gentle throat therapy by Luckies; testimonial campaign at the end of the thirties.

was to become the most expensive promotional campaign in the history of merchandising – one in which Raymond Loewy was eventually to play his own stylish part.

In 1925 George Washington Hill succeeded his father, Percival S. Hill, as the President of the American Tobacco Company. He made it his single-minded business to promote *Lucky Strike*, the latecomer in premium branded, blended cigarettes (after *Camels* and *Chesterfield*), from Number Three to Number One. Design had not yet been discovered as a means of stimulating sales, so *Luckies* used promotions. In 1923 a skywriting campaign spelt-out "Lucky Strike" 10,000 feet above 122 US cities; the corner of Broadway and 45th Street there was a permanent exhibit showing how *Lucky Strikes* were made; the *Lucky Strike Radio Hour* that debuted over thirty-nine NBC radio stations in September 1928, revolutionised advertising and, incidentally, gave rise to the expression "hit parade". In the forties it was presented by a young singer called Frank Sinatra.

"Are you inhaling?" A frank discussion on a "taboo theme" is promised by this advertisement from the early fifties.

The Beauties and the Beast

Like *Coca-Cola*, *Lucky Strike* achieved prominence by using celebrity endorsements from women vaudeville stars. (In this style, Princess Marie of Roumania endorsed Ponds cold cream which brought her a rebuke in her native country). Going one step further, an early novelty of Albert D. Lasker's Lord & Thomas'[3] agency *Lucky Strike* ads was, following *Camels'* precedent, the sensational use of testimonials from women. Celebrities included both exotic opera singers and domestic Americans: aviatrix Amelia Earheart was one, Florence Easton, a Metropolitan Opera prima donna, was another, movie actress Jean Harlow (of whom Dorothy Parker asked: Is that Harlow with a 't'?") yet another. In ads which appeared in 1927, Easton apparently believed that *Lucky Strikes* were actually good for her throat. [4] The modern cigarette had met the modern woman.

Having taken on his tobacco rivals, Hill next decided to confront the US confectionary industry, using the advertising copyline "Reach for a *Lucky*, instead of a sweet" [5] (inspired by the sight in those innocent times of a fat black woman eating sweets on a street corner while an elegant slim white woman whooshed past smoking in her chauffeur-driven limo). With impressive hubris, Hill presented *Luckies* as a slimming aid. Some New York stores, including Schrafft's, took *Lucky Strikes* off their shelves in protest and the confectionery industry made a formal complaint to the Federal Trade Commission (FTC). These were days when cigarettes could be aggressively promoted [6] and George Washington Hill was not squeamish about his spending: *Lucky Strike* became the most extravagant client in the US advertising business.

The relentless promotion of *Lucky Strike* won a considerable market share for the American Tobacco Company and in a counter-attack, in March 1930 alone the rival R. J. Reynolds Company spent 300,000 US dollars supporting *Camels* and attacking *Lucky Strike*: the cigarette wars long preceded the *Cola* Wars. The same year *Lucky Strike* became the leading US cigarette brand.

A young star on the air: Frank "the Voice" Sinatra on the road to success with *Lucky Strike* at the beginning of the fifties.

Promotions and celebrity endorsements at first played a bigger part in *Lucky Strike's* sales success than packaging design, but there had been contact with great artists before Raymond Loewy's distinctive design was brought-in to supplement the battery of other marketing services employed by the American Tobacco Company. Between 1920 and 1928, while cigars and pipe tobacco fell by 20% and 9% respectively, cigarette sales rose by 123%. Then bad times followed good: the Wall Street crash of '29 meant that ads had to be produced in black and white as an economy measure, but the photographs used were by Edward Steichen.

"Reach for a Lucky instead" – advertising in the age of ignorance (around 1930).

Lucky Strike had been launched with a simple green pack. Probably the work of an anonymous 'commercial artist', it had become a successful and familiar icon of vernacular American business, thanks in part to the efforts of American Tobacco Company's PR consultant, Edward L. Bernays. One of the pioneers of his own profession, since 1920 Bernays had realised that in a continent lacking an *Almanach de Gotha*, brands provide cultural stability and continuity.

Luckies was by the mid thirties an American Standard Brand, but the ambitious and restless George Washington Hill wanted more. Bernays found Hill's behaviour "aggressive" and said he "swaggered round his office, his arms swinging. At the slightest provocation he exploded, his face purpling with rage".[7] Hill was a landmark client, quite beyond parody. Pugnacious, crass and singleminded. To emphasise the importance of hard-hitting ads he would make a forlorn copywriter stand in front of his desk holding a heavy statue while he busied himself at his desk, then would explain his copylines were just as leaden. He once knocked a glass of water into someone's lap by way of illustration, saying "you won't forget that".

Hill inhaled four packs of *Luckies* a day and had packages taped to the back window of his *Rolls-Royce* and silhouettes of the pack on each tail-light. His dachsunds were called Lucky and Strike. He had tried everything to promote *Lucky Strike* to its commercial dominance. Everything, that is, except design. But now was the moment that Raymond Loewy – pioneer industrial designer – was, with Edward L. Bernays and Albert Lasker, drafted in to complete the line-up of marketing services available to Lucky Strike.

In the daily struggle against the "frog", prima donna Florence Easton swears to *Luckies* (1927).

A brilliant makeover

By 1941 Raymond Loewy's curriculum vitae looked like this: 1929, first major industrial design commission, styling a duplicator for Sigmund Gestetner; 1933, first commissions for Sears Roebuck, Pennsylvania Railroad and Greyhound Corporation; 1934 *Huppmobile* goes on sale, Loewy opens a London office; 1937, designs Lord & Taylor interiors; 1938 begins collaboration with Studebaker and *Coca-Cola*; 1939 designs Chrysler Motors Building at New York's World Fair. He was probably the best known, and certainly the most effectively promoted, designer in the world. The actual means is not recorded, but it's a fair guess that either Bernays or Lasker introduced Loewy to Hill.

Florence Easton,
Metropolitan prima donna,
ever cautious of her lovely voice,

© Mishkin, N. Y.

writes:

"Singers must be cautious regarding their throats. Like other singers, I prefer Lucky Strikes because they are never irritating and because of their finer flavor."

You, too, will find that Lucky Strikes are mild and mellow—the finest cigarettes you ever smoked, made of the finest Turkish and domestic tobaccos, properly aged and blended with great skill, _and_ there is an extra process—"It's toasted"— no harshness, not a bit of bite.

"It's toasted"
Your Throat Protection

Smoke a LUCKY
to feel your LEVEL best!

Luckies' fine tobacco picks you up when you're low . . . calms you down when you're tense—puts you on the Lucky level! That's why it's so important to remember that LUCKY STRIKE MEANS FINE TOBACCO —mild, ripe, light tobacco. No wonder more independent tobacco experts—auctioneers, buyers and warehousemen—smoke Luckies regularly than the next two leading brands combined! Get a carton of Luckies today!

L.S/M.F.T. — *Lucky Strike Means Fine Tobacco*

So round, so firm, so fully packed — so free and easy on the draw

In *Never Leave Well Enough Alone*, his wonderful, self-dramatizing autobiography, Loewy describes the encounter with positively Hollywood bravura and stylish reference to psychologically telling detail. [8] The way Loewy tells it, Hill called into his office one day in 1941. He took off his jacket, but kept on his hat, a battered garment used to store fishing flies. Taking out his cigarette case and lighter, Loewy was told that they were by the Parisian jeweller de luxe, Cartier. Loewy had probably noticed already. The designer responded by flashing his own bespoke Cartier suspenders. Passionate consumers each, the men bonded.

Hill had been persuaded that Loewy, the master of industrial transformations was the man needed to design – or, rather, redesign – the *Lucky Strike* packet. The original green packet, while comfortingly familiar, looked drab and un-modern. With his record of stylish transformations of dull machinery into swanky style, it was a job with Loewy's name on it. His fee proposal came in the form of a typically stylish gesture: a bet of 50,000 US dollars on success or failure. The betting slip was one of George Washington Hill's business cards.

Loewy, in full accordance with the myth and reality of his own legend, produced another classic transformation. Loewy replaced the classic green ground (which some thought had unattractive associations with the military) with white and made the pack symmetrical and identical, front and back. [9] He turned the established circular motif into a much stronger target device, used front and rear. He sharpened up the typography, giving

LUCKY STRIKE MEANS FINE TOBACCO!

"Scouting the crop before auctions open." Painted from life on a Southern farm by Georges Schreiber

So Round, So Firm, So Fully Packed—So Free and Easy On The Draw

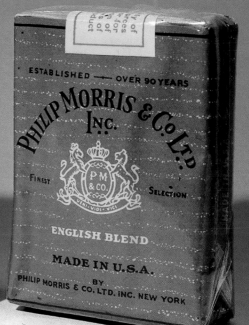

it more air, and gave the whole a clarity and modernity which meant that, in all essentials, the *Lucky Strike* packet of 1998 is unimproved over Loewy's 1941 design. Simple stuff – a brilliant makeover. It was suddenly modern. It wasn't, of course, true that (like the *Coke* bottle) you could recognise it in the dark, but the new *Luckies* pack did satisfy Loewy's claim that you could recognise it from any direction.

Just as The *Coca-Cola* Company won global distribution on the back of the US war effort after chairman Robert Woodruff's claim that every GI should have daily access to his five cents *Coke*, so *Lucky Strike* travelled with the military and gained access to world markets. Like *Coke*, *Luckies* became a symbol of American prosperity and well-being. In Germany from 1945, *Lucky Strike* was even a substitute currency until the reforms of 1948. A cultural inheritance of this is that even today, *Lucky Strike* has a more prominent position in the German market than anywhere else in Europe.

For a designer of Loewy's disposition a package was the best expression of his flamboyant genius. Famously associated with the meretricious application of stream-lining to a deskbound pencil-sharpener (which, in fact, never actually went into production), Loewy knew nothing about the actual science of aerodynamics. Surface style was his subject, as Loewy himself put it in his autobiography.

Lucky Strike **pack for the US-American troops overseas, around 1945. Next to it, the competition's product from Philip Morris.**

A true classic

No-one caught the mood of industrial America at mid-century better than Raymond Loewy. He wanted to get in on the act, so rewrote a part of the script for him to play himself. Loewy loved what he saw in America and wanted to claim part of it, but in his enthusiasm he sometimes overstated his case. One imagines that Loewy felt like PR pioneer, Benjamin Sonnenberg:

"Here is the phenomenon of a young immigrant who, while he willy-nilly is dumped on the eastern seabord of the United States, through a process of experiences becomes more American than *Coca-Cola* and assimilates himself to the point of knowing the latest boogie-woogie beat in the propaganda of his times. I could have sold rugs in Stamboul, but I became a ballyhoo artist. I was meant to operate from Baghdad to Trafalgar Square. I brought to America a kind of freshness but assimilated America's *Coca-Cola* idiom. It's as though Paderewski became a Joe diMaggio, or Rachmaninoff took to chewing gum on the stage and twirling a lasso, the way Will Rogers did." [10]

Raymond Loewy decided to renew the world, so designed himself a career. It is fascinating to compare the energetically articulated myth with the less well publicised reality. Take the *Coldspot* refrigerator of 1936, one of Loewy's restlessly publicised transformations which, in accordance with the myth of industrial design's power to increase profit, was cited as proof of the efficacy of

Gestetner *Salutes*

RAYMOND LOEWY

WORLD'S MOST RENOWNED INDUSTRIAL DESIGNER

Gestetner adds its voice to the chorus of tributes paid to the world's most gifted industrial designer RAYMOND LOEWY and notes with pride that he began his remarkable career by re-designing the Gestetner decades ago— in 1929.

1908

1929
RAYMOND LOEWY'S FIRST
INDUSTRIAL DESIGN

TODAY
THE LATEST DESIGN-PRODUCT OF
THE RAYMOND LOEWY STUDIOS

Shake hands with L.S. Green

L.S./M.F.T. Lucky Strike is the brand that made fine tobacco famous.
And it's making a name for menthol, too.

the Loewy method. Certainly, Loewy did a superb styling job on the fridge, transforming a banale object by application of auto industry styling motifs into an attractive consumer durable. Every article about Loewy routinely repeated the designer's own estimate that after his re-working sales had increased to 275,000 annually against 60,000 previously. No evidence was ever vouchsafed for this and three years later Loewy went to work for rival, *Frigidaire*.

Loewy's name has often been linked to the design of the *Coca-Cola* bottle, in fact the work of an obscure glass engineer called Alexander Samuelson circa 1916. An interview in *Life* magazine [11] is the source of the confusion about authorship of the *Coke* bottle, a confusion Loewy never did anything to correct. Indeed, his decision to describe the kicked-up haunches of his *Studebaker Avanti* as "the *Coke* bottle look" seemed to imply ownership. Certainly, Loewy never spoke an untruth about his relationship with *Coca-Cola*, although he did not mind misleading his public. The *Coca-Cola* archives in Atlanta reveal the extent of his true relationship with the Company: US Patent Office No.145,222, a refrigerator and US Patent Office No.149,656, the famous counter-top dispenser. The relationship was summarised by *Coke's* one-time Manager of Graphic Arts, Marshall H. Lane:

"He was retained to study and recommend designs for our ice-box coolers. His firm of designers did a commendable job. Off and on through the years they and other designers have been called in to work on other projects". [12]

Lucky Strike occurred at a moment when US business was maturing and, as a direct consequence, the design profession had evolved from the artisan commercial artist to the professional consultant. Raymond Loewy was a leader of this new profession which soon took its place alongside the older established marketing services of advertising and PR.

Lucky Strike also characterises another aspect of the design phenomenon: it was not the work of a designer alone. What was required was a megalomaniac client and ingenious PR or advertising. Design was an adjunct to these professions. But while Loewy was often tempted to overstate the rôle in business of autonomous creativity (especially his own) the totemic success of the *Lucky Strike* package design had proved his point and made his mark for the profession he did so much to establish:

"*Luckies*, aided by their sublime package, are a true classic" [13].

Today's hard pack that's on the market in addition to the classical soft pack.

LUCKIES
AMERICAN BLEND

LUCKY
STRIKE

IT'S TOASTED

FILTERS

DIE EG-GESUNDHEITSMINISTER:
RAUCHEN GEFÄHRDET
DIE GESUNDHEIT

"Light my Lucky."

Notes

1 Although, according to Stuart Berg Flexner in *I Hear America Talking* (1976), the expression "49er" did not become popular until later and no recorded mention of it exists before 1853.

2 Joseph C. Robert: *The Story of Tobacco in America*, University of North Carolina Press, Chapel Hill, 1967, p. 233.

3 Lord & Thomas was a pioneer of the "Reason Why" salesmanship technique: the beginning of scientific advertising.

4 Not everyone viewed the phenomenon favourably. The graphics trade journal *Printer's Ink* had warned in 1919 against the "insidious campaign to create women smokers".

5 Apparently inspired by Lydia E. Pinkham's more wholesome 1891 campaign „Reach for a vegetable instead of a sweet".

6 As late as the mid fifties, there was by no means a consensus, even among medical professionals, that cigarette smoking was lethal. W. Koskowski's authoritative *The Habit of Tobacco Smoking*, Staples Press, London, 1955, is sceptical about a direct link between smoking and lung, oesophageal and mouth carcinomas.

7 Stephen Fox: *The Mirror Makers – a history of American advertising and its creators* ,Vintage Books, New York, 1985, p. 115.

8 Raymond Loewy: *Never Leave Well Enough Alone*, Simon and Schuster, New York, 1951, p. 145.

9 The transformation from green to white was not purely aesthetic: high chromium content made the old green ink uneconomical during the War.

10 Isadore Barmash: Live Better Than Your Clients: *The Fabulous Life and Times of Benjamin Sonnenberg*, America s Greatest Publicist, Dodd, New York, 1983, p. 21.

11 John Kolber: "The Great Packager", *Life*, May, 1949, pp. 110 ff.

12 ms. Correspondence, 29th October 1970, Marshall H. Lane. *Coca-Cola* Company Archives.

13 Richard Sexton: *American Style – Classic Product Design from Airstream to Zippo*, Chronicle Books, San Francisco, 1987, p. 15.

Photo Credits
pp 2, 5, 6: Laurence Loewy; p 28: archive and collection Hans-Georg Böcher, Wiesbaden; all other images: Verlag form

Preceding double page: left the green camouflage to the military and now presents itself in white – first advertisement for the *Lucky Strike* in the new Loewy outfit (1941).

Left: US-advertisement for the Light version (1980).

Following double page and subsequent pictures: since the early nineties most likely one of the most successful advertising campaigns – the *Lucky Strike*, still in the Loewy outfit, on a new road to success.

Here comes the sun.

Lucky Strike. Sonst nichts.

Ooh, what a night...

Lucky Strike. Sonst nichts.

British American Tobacco
(Germany) GmbH
Alsterufer 4
D-20354 Hamburg
Fon +49 (0) 40 41 51 - 01
Fax +49 (0) 40 41 51 - 3231

Lucky Strikes Back.

Haben Sie

1

2

1

Ihre Buntstifte dabei?

Lucky Strike. Sonst nichts.

Service

If you would like to receive our catalog,
please contact us:

Verlag form.
Books & Magazines on design issues.

Telephone +49 (0) 69 94 33 25-0
Facsimile   +49 (0) 69 94 33 25-25
e-Mail: form@form.de
http://WWW.form.de

Impressum

©1998 Verlag form GmbH,
Frankfurt am Main
All rights reserved, especially those of
translation into other languages.

Editor:
Volker Fischer

Editorial Department:
Anne Hamilton

Graphic Design:
Sarah Dorkenwald,
Absatz, Gesellschaft für
Kommunikations-Design,
Frankfurt am Main

Lithography:
Hans Altenkirch
Mediaproduktionen GmbH,
Nieder-Olm

Print:
Franz Spiegel Buch GmbH,
Ulm

Die Deutsche Bibliothek –
CIP-Einheitsaufnahme

The Lucky Strike packet by
Raymond Loewy / Stephen Bayley.
[Ed.: Volker Fischer]. –
Frankfurt am Main : Verl. Form, 1998
(Design classics)
Dt. Ausg. u.d.T.: Die Lucky-Strike-
Packung von Raymond Loewy
ISBN 3-931317-72-2